The Genius Of THE ANGLO-SAXONS

INNOVATIONS FROM PAST CIVILIZATIONS

IZZI HOWELL

CRABTREE
PUBLISHING COMPANY
WWW.CRABTREEBOOKS.COM

CRABTREE
PUBLISHING COMPANY
WWW.CRABTREEBOOKS.COM

Published in Canada
Crabtree Publishing
616 Welland Avenue
St. Catharines, ON
L2M 5V6

Published in the United States
Crabtree Publishing
PMB 59051
350 Fifth Ave, 59th Floor
New York, NY 10118

Published in 2020 by Crabtree Publishing Company

First published in Great Britain in 2019 by The Watts Publishing Group
Copyright © The Watts Publishing Group 2019

Author: Izzi Howell

Editorial director: Kathy Middleton

Editors: Izzi Howell, Petrice Custance

Proofreader: Melissa Boyce

Series designer: Rocket Design (East Anglia) Ltd

Prepress technician: Tammy McGarr

Print coordinator: Katherine Berti

Consultant: Philip Parker

The website addresses (URLs) included in this book were valid at the time of going to press. However, it is possible that contents or addresses may have changed since the publication of this book. No responsibility for any such changes can be accepted by either the author or the Publisher.

Printed in the U.S.A./072019/CG20190501

Photo credits:
Alamy: Granger Historical Picture Archive cover, The History Collection 9, David Lyons 12, INTERFOTO 20, Timewatch Images 23b; Getty: duncan1890 5, 7b and 25l, dan_wrench 7t, Grafissimo 8b, Jean Williamson/LOOP IMAGES 11t, Dorling Kindersley 13t, 14 and 30–31, Ashmolean Museum/Heritage Images 15, lightphoto 17t, Florilegius/SSPL 17b and 29, whitemay 21t, Wellwoods 27t, Historical Picture Archive/Corbis 27b, empire331 28; Metropolitan Museum: Gift of J. Pierpont Morgan, 1917 3t and 16 (all), Purchase, Joseph Pulitzer Bequest, 1987 4l and 26b, Purchase, Rogers Fund, and Alastair B. Martin, Levy Hermanos Foundation Inc. and J. William Middendorf II Gifts, 1985 25r; Portable Antiquities Scheme: Salisbury and South Wiltshire Museum 18t, 18b; Shutterstock: Peter Lorimer title page and 10, Awe Inspiring Images 4b and 19, Morphart Creation 8t, Peter Hermes Furian 11b, Simon Annable 15b, azure1 21bl, Coprid 21br, Nataly Studio 22t, Dionisvera 22c, AlexAvich 22b, Vadim Petrakov 23t, Magdalena Wielobob 24t, pullia 24c, yul38885 24b, Daniel Buxton photography 26t; Stefan Chabluk 4r.
Images on title page and 10 taken at West Stow Anglo-Saxon village.

All design elements from Shutterstock.

Every attempt has been made to clear copyright. Should there be any inadvertent omission please apply to the publisher for rectification.

Library and Archives Canada Cataloguing in Publication

Title: The genius of the Anglo-Saxons / Izzi Howell.
Names: Howell, Izzi, author.
Series: Genius of the ancients.
Description: Series statement: The genius of the ancients | Includes index.
Identifiers: Canadiana (print) 20190108339 | Canadiana (ebook) 20190108347 | ISBN 9780778765738 (hardcover) | ISBN 9780778765936 (softcover) | ISBN 9781427123909 (HTML)
Subjects: LCSH: Civilization, Anglo-Saxon—Juvenile literature. | LCSH: Technological innovations—Great Britain—History—To 1500—Juvenile literature. | LCSH: Technological innovations—Great Britain—Juvenile literature. | LCSH: Anglo-Saxons—Juvenile literature. | LCSH: Great Britain—History—Anglo-Saxon period, 449-1066—Juvenile literature.
Classification: LCC DA152.2 .H69 2019 | DDC j942.01—dc23

Library of Congress Cataloging-in-Publication Data

Names: Howell, Izzi, author.
Title: The genius of the Anglo-Saxons / Izzi Howell.
Description: New York, New York : Crabtree Publishing Company, 2020. | Series: The genius of the ancients | Audience: Ages: 9-12. | Audience: Grades: 4-6. | Includes index. |
Identifiers: LCCN 2019014236 (print) | LCCN 2019018663 (ebook) | ISBN 9781427123909 (Electronic) | ISBN 9780778765738 (hardcover) | ISBN 9780778765936 (pbk.)
Subjects: LCSH: Civilization, Anglo-Saxon--Juvenile literature. | Technological innovations--Great Britain--Juvenile literature. | Anglo-Saxons--Juvenile literature. | Great Britain--History--Anglo-Saxon period, 449-1066--Juvenile literature.
Classification: LCC DA152.2 (ebook) | LCC DA152.2 .H695 2020 (print) | DDC 942.01--dc23
LC record available at https://lccn.loc.gov/2019014236

CONTENTS

THE ANGLO-SAXONS

Who?

In 410, after the Romans left England, Anglo-Saxons began invading and settling the land. They were mainly made up of three different groups: the Angles, the Jutes, and the Saxons from what is now Germany, Denmark, and the Netherlands. Different Anglo-Saxon groups took over different parts of England, defeating some of the **Celtic** tribes living there and pushing others into Wales and Scotland. It was a time of great change, with fighting between Anglo-Saxon kingdoms and the Celtic tribes, as well as **Viking** raids from the late 700s. However, for the Anglo-Saxon **civilization**, it was also a period of **culture**, art, and learning.

This map shows the route of the Angle, Jute, and Saxon settlers.

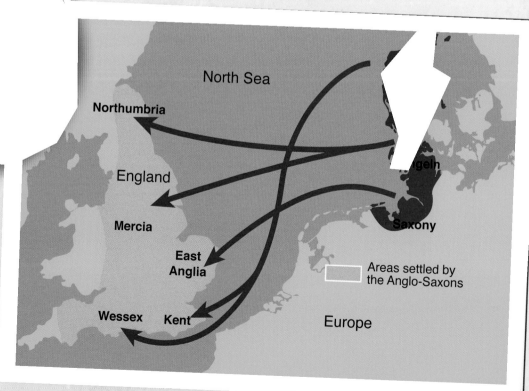

North Sea

Northumbria

England

Mercia

East Anglia

Wessex   Kent

Angeln

Saxony

Europe

Areas settled by the Anglo-Saxons

Anglo-Saxon jewelry and weapons were often decorated with **intricate** details and inlaid with colorful stones.

What happened?

At first, Anglo-Saxon England was divided into kingdoms and ruled by different kings. Over time, some kingdoms became more powerful than others. However, all Anglo-Saxon kingdoms faced a common enemy—the Vikings from Scandinavia. In 886, after years of attacks, the Anglo-Saxons allowed the Vikings to rule over an area of northern and western England called the Danelaw. This was the beginning of a period of power-sharing between the Anglo-Saxons and the Vikings. There were periods when the Vikings ruled over all of England, but the Anglo-Saxons took back control several times.

The Anglo-Saxon age ended with the arrival of a new group of invaders—the Normans from France. The last Anglo-Saxon king, Harold Godwinson, was defeated in battle by the Normans, led by William the Conqueror. In 1066, William became the new Norman king of England. We can still see the **legacy** of the Anglo-Saxons today in the English language and landscape.

Harold Godwinson, the last Anglo-Saxon king, died at the Battle of Hastings in 1066. According to some reports, he was shot in the head with an arrow.

KINGDOMS AND RULERS

GENIUS LAND SHARING

When the Anglo-Saxons arrived in England, they were not a united group. Different groups of Anglo-Saxons settled in different areas, which then became separate kingdoms.

Lots of leaders

Each early Anglo-Saxon kingdom was ruled by its own leader. These leaders made decisions about how their kingdom was run. However, this system didn't last long. Over time, larger kingdoms took over smaller ones until there were only seven large kingdoms. Sometimes, the king of one of these seven kingdoms became more powerful than the others and had influence over them. However, no king ever succeeded in uniting the seven kingdoms.

This map shows the kingdoms in Anglo-Saxon England in around 750.

Celts
Anglo-Saxons

0 40 80 120 km

NORTHUMBRIA

North Sea

Irish Sea

MERCIA

WALES

EAST ANGLIA

ESSEX

WESSEX

KENT

SUSSEX

English Channel

FRANCE

6

Offa's Dyke was a 59-foot (18 m) tall bank of earth next to a ditch. It can still be seen today in places such as Shropshire, England.

ATHELSTAN.

One king

The Vikings conquered all the Anglo-Saxon kingdoms except Wessex. From Wessex, the Anglo-Saxons fought back and recaptured most of England. The first Anglo-Saxon king to control the whole of England was Athelstan. Under his rule, the Anglo-Saxons took back Viking-controlled York, making Athelstan the ruler of the entire country. However, Anglo-Saxon kingdoms still kept many of their own **customs**, even though they were all now ruled by the same king. This made the shift from separate kingdoms to a unified country easier for people.

Athelstan ruled from 924 to 939. After his death, the Vikings recaptured part of the north of England. The Anglo-Saxons didn't rule the whole of England again until the 950s.

SOCIETY

The king was the most powerful person in Anglo-Saxon **society**. However, kings also had to think about the needs of everyone in the kingdom and listen to the advice of **noblemen**.

GENIUS
★ KIND KINGS ★

Different people

Anglo-Saxon society was a **hierarchy** in order of importance, wealth, and power. Kings were at the top, followed by rich and powerful noblemen. Beneath them were skilled craftspeople and merchants, and then farmers and laborers. Enslaved people were at the bottom. Women across the hierarchy had very few rights.

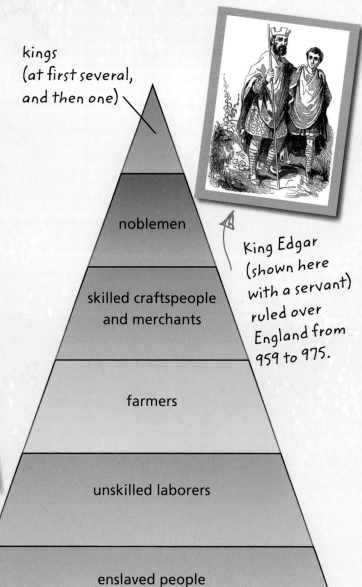

kings
(at first several,
and then one)

noblemen

skilled craftspeople
and merchants

farmers

unskilled laborers

enslaved people

King Edgar
(shown here
with a servant)
ruled over
England from
959 to 975.

Farmers used simple
plows to prepare the
soil for planting.

Helping each other

Anglo-Saxon kings benefited from the people in their kingdoms. They could call on all men to fight in battle and received some money from taxes. The kings also worked for the people. They protected the kingdom from invasion and acted as judges to sort out people's problems. After a battle, kings shared any land or treasure won with the important people in their kingdom to keep them happy and loyal.

This image from an Anglo-Saxon translation of a religious text shows an Anglo-Saxon king surrounded by the Witan.

(((BRAIN WAVE)))

Anglo-Saxon kings had to listen to the advice of a council of noblemen and religious leaders called the Witan. This stopped kings from having too much power. The Witan gave kings suggestions on laws and taxes, and helped the king choose who would become king after he died.

WOW!

Occasionally, the Witan removed bad kings from power who weren't ruling fairly!

VILLAGES

The Romans left behind several towns and cities with stone buildings. However, the Anglo-Saxons did not live as the Romans did. The Anglo-Saxons built new settlements that suited their farming lifestyle, leaving most of the Roman towns to fall into ruin and eventually disappear.

GENIUS ★ FARMERS' HOMES ★

The right location

Most Anglo-Saxons were farmers. People needed to be spread out across the land so that everyone could have their own space for farming. The Anglo-Saxons built many small villages across England. They chose spots near the **natural resources** they would need to survive, such as wood for construction, fresh water, and **fertile** land for crops.

This reconstruction of an Anglo-Saxon house is made from wood, with a **thatched** straw roof.

TEST OF TIME

Many towns in England were settled in Anglo-Saxon times. These towns often have **Old English** words in their names. For example, "ham" and "ton" are the sources of the words home and town. The Old English words are still found in names such as Birmingham and Southampton.

The interior of this reconstructed Anglo-Saxon hall shows benches where villagers could sit during a feast.

"Wich" was an Anglo-Saxon word for a trading settlement. Today, it still appears in the names of cities, such as Ipswich and Norwich.

Houses and halls

Anglo-Saxon villages were small and simple, as farmers did not have the time or money to build large, fancy homes. Most people lived in small wooden huts with thatched roofs. There was just one room inside the house, where an entire family would eat, sleep, and spend time together. The biggest building in the village was the hall, where the village chief lived.

Village to town

Over time, some Anglo-Saxon villages grew into larger towns. These towns were home to people with different professions, such as skilled craftspeople and traders, not just local farmers. Later, defensive walls were added around some of these towns to protect residents from Viking attacks.

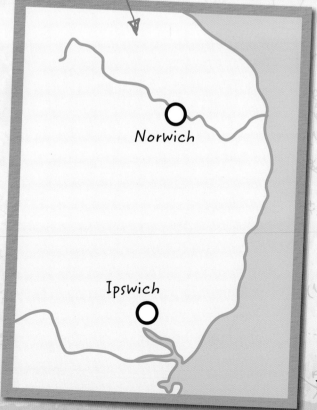

Norwich

Ipswich

DEFENSE

When the Anglo-Saxons invaded England in the 400s, their focus was on attacking areas to gain land. Once they settled in England, defense became much more important to the Anglo-Saxons, especially when the Vikings began raiding their villages.

GENIUS
KEEPING SAFE

Part-time armies

The various Anglo-Saxon kingdoms occasionally fought each other. They also faced attacks from Celtic people, such as the Picts from Scotland. However, these attacks were uncommon enough that full-time armies weren't needed. It was more important for men to work full-time as farmers than as soldiers. If a kingdom was under threat, all men in the area left their jobs to serve in a fyrd, which was a temporary army that formed whenever it became necessary.

Many historians believe these carved stones found in Scotland show a battle between the Picts and Anglo-Saxons from Northumbria. The stones were carved by the Picts.

TEST of TIME

Today, most countries have a permanent army made up of professional soldiers. However, some countries also have backup soldiers who do not serve full-time. For example, in England today, people can volunteer in the Army Reserve. They keep their normal jobs, but can be called into the army in an emergency.

A new system

In the 800s, Viking attacks became more frequent. Because it took time for men to leave their villages and assemble for the fyrd, they were not able to respond quickly enough to these attacks. To solve this problem, King Alfred created a permanent Anglo-Saxon army, which was always ready for battle. He also set up a navy to patrol the coastline and defend it against ships carrying Viking warriors.

King Alfred stationed navy ships to defend the coastline and respond quickly to a Viking attack.

Defense forts

King Alfred also ordered the construction of new **fortified** defensive structures called burhs, where people could hide during Viking attacks. Some burhs were walled towns left behind by the Romans. Others were new sites built in areas likely to be attacked by Vikings, such as coastlines. The burhs were connected by a network of roads so that people and messages could easily travel between them.

An Anglo-Saxon burh contained houses and other buildings, such as workshops, surrounded by banks of earth lined with stones for support. Wooden spikes were placed on top of the banks to stop people from climbing over.

WOW!

The city of Oxford began as a burh built on Alfred's orders. This fortified settlement was in an important position at the point where two major rivers cross.

WEAPONS AND ARMOR

Men who were called to serve in the fyrd had to supply their own weapons and armor. These men came from every part of Anglo-Saxon society, both rich and poor, which meant that many different types of equipment were used in battle.

Cheap and effective

Most fyrd soldiers were poor farmers or laborers, so they didn't have much money to spend on equipping themselves for battle. They made the best weapons and armor they could afford to keep themselves safe. Spears were the most common weapons as they were cheap and easy to produce. Soldiers also used axes and knives for close-up **combat**. They protected themselves with leather armor and a simple circular wooden shield.

Historians think that Anglo-Saxon shields were sometimes painted with colorful patterns and designs.

(((BRAIN WAVE)))

Anglo-Saxon shields had a circular metal panel in the middle. This protected the weak center of the shield and stopped it from breaking apart when hit.

High-class weapons

Richer soldiers could afford more powerful weapons and protective armor. They fought with sharp metal swords, which could do a lot of damage with just one blow. Swords were so valuable that they were often passed down from father to son. To protect themselves, wealthier soldiers wore metal helmets and chain mail, a form of armor made from hundreds of tiny metal rings joined together.

Battlefield tactics

Although fyrd soldiers had different weapons and armor, they were one united army on the battlefield. A popular battle tactic was to put their shields together to create a wall. This protected the front line of soldiers, while the army moved forward together. Some of the soldiers would run out in front of the wall to get **momentum** to throw spears at the enemy, before quickly running back behind the wall for protection.

These are the remains of an Anglo-Saxon sword that was buried with its owner. Like many Anglo-Saxon objects, it is decorated with patterns.

These people are taking part in a **reenactment** of an Anglo-Saxon battle. Most Anglo-Saxon soldiers fought on foot.

15

TRADE

After the Anglo-Saxons settled in England, they were still connected to their homelands, such as present-day Germany and Denmark, and the rest of Europe through trade. The Anglo-Saxons traded many goods, including luxury items such as jewelry.

Sharing locally

Most Anglo-Saxon trade was between kingdoms within England. Fish from rivers and seas were brought inland. People also traded **raw materials**, such as wool and metal, and crafted objects, such as jewelry, weapons, glassware, and pottery. Some kingdoms sent crafted objects abroad, where they were bought by rich and important people.

This glass jar and these brooches were probably made in Anglo-Saxon Kent. However, they were all found in other European countries. The jar was found in Germany and the brooches in France. This shows how far away the Anglo-Saxons traded.

Sutton Hoo treasures

Beginning in 1939, many Anglo-Saxon objects were found in a burial ground called Sutton Hoo, on the eastern coast of England. An important king or warrior and his entire ship had been buried there. Also buried were luxury traded items from overseas, such as silver bowls from the eastern Mediterranean, drinking horns from Europe, and copper bowls from Celtic people in Ireland or Wales. Only the richest Anglo-Saxons could have afforded such valuable objects.

))) BRAIN WAVE)))

Even within England, the Anglo-Saxons transported items for trade by ship. They found it was much faster and safer to travel by water than by land. Their small ships could sail up rivers, quickly carrying them inland. They also used these ships to travel to Europe and along the European coastline.

This is a replica of a helmet found at Sutton Hoo. It is similar to other helmets from the same time found in Sweden.

This Anglo-Saxon ship is powered by sails. Sailors also used oars to power ships when close to shore.

LAWS

At first, each Anglo-Saxon king and his advisers made laws for their kingdom. Each kingdom had different laws. Later, a more unified legal system was established. Similar laws were then followed by different kingdoms across England.

GENIUS
COMMUNITY LAW

Following the rules

Ordinary Anglo-Saxons played an important role in ensuring that laws were followed. They all made a promise not to break the law, and to report anyone who did. This meant that the king and his noblemen didn't need to spend time looking out for lawbreakers. People who broke their promise were punished with fines or even **exile**.

Anglo-Saxon coins

Weregild

In Anglo-Saxon times, the victim of a crime could claim money from the person who had committed it. This money was known as weregild. The amount of weregild depended on the seriousness of the crime. The largest amount was paid to the family of a murder victim. This system was seen as a fair and simple way to punish criminals and make things right for their victims.

WOW!

Weregild fines also depended on the position of the victim in Anglo-Saxon society. If a nobleman was murdered, his family would receive much more weregild than the family of a murdered farmer.

New influences

As kings started to rule over more than one area, they were able to pick and choose the laws they wanted from different kingdoms and combine them into new laws. After many Anglo-Saxons **converted** to **Christianity** in the 600s, new ideas about law based on Christian thinking were also introduced. The laws of the Vikings in the Danelaw inspired the Anglo-Saxons to develop legal traditions, such as selecting men to sit on a **jury** to decide if someone was guilty of a crime.

King Alfred the Great was famous for introducing a law code that combined Anglo-Saxon laws with Christian teaching.

TEST OF TIME

Anglo-Saxon and Viking juries were the first in the world. Today, juries are used in most countries to provide a balanced opinion of court cases.

OLD ENGLISH

The Anglo-Saxons spoke Old English, a Germanic language they brought with them to England. This replaced the Celtic languages and Latin spoken in England previously. Old English is one of the roots of the modern English language.

GENIUS OF LEARNING

Changing alphabets

Old English was originally written in the **rune** alphabet. The Anglo-Saxon rune alphabet is known as the futhorc, as F, U, TH, O, R, and C (see panel at right) were the sounds of the first six runes in the alphabet. Later, the Anglo-Saxons began using an early version of the Latin alphabet, which is similar to the one we use today. Experts use Anglo-Saxon texts written in runes or in the Latin alphabet to learn more about this period of history.

ᚠ ᚢ ᚦ ᚩ ᚱ ᚳ
F U TH O R C

This chest from the 700s is carved from whalebone and decorated with runes. It also shows scenes from an old Germanic legend (left) and from Christian teaching (right).

Old English for all

Old English was mostly just a spoken language until the reign of King Alfred. Latin was used for religious and academic texts, but few people knew how to read or write in any language. However, Alfred had a great interest in learning. He encouraged more people to learn how to read Old English. He also requested that books be written in Old English instead of Latin. This meant that more people could understand them and become educated.

Alfred only learned how to read as an adult, but he was passionate about education and **literacy**.

TEST OF TIME

One-third of Old English words survive today in modern English. They are often short words that are connected to the natural world or the human body, such as apple, gold, and eye.

))) BRAIN WAVE)))

Anglo-Saxons were very creative with language. They used kennings, which were a combination of two words to make a new word. Kennings were used in poetry and storytelling to interest the audience and as a fun way to play with words. Some kennings include "wave floater" to mean ship, and "bone house" to describe the human body!

Old English — netle
Modern English — nettle

Old English — fether
Modern English — feather

FOOD

For ordinary people, food had to be simple and cheap. However, the richest Anglo-Saxons could afford extravagant feasts of the finest food and drink.

GENIUS MEALS FOR ALL

Plant life

The diet of ordinary Anglo-Saxons was mostly made up of plants that grew well in the cool, wet English **climate**. They ate vegetables, such as onions, carrots, and cabbages, and grains, such as oats, barley, and wheat. Occasionally, they had access to small amounts of meat from pigs, cows, and sheep.

Anglo-Saxon farmers grew crops such as oats and peas.

(((BRAIN WAVE)))

It was too dangerous to drink freshwater in Anglo-Saxon times, as the water wasn't treated to remove germs. Instead, the Anglo-Saxons drank weak beer. The process of making beer killed the germs in the water, so it was much safer to drink.

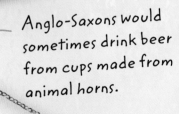

Anglo-Saxons would sometimes drink beer from cups made from animal horns.

Busy schedules

Anglo-Saxon women were responsible for preparing food. However, they also had to clean, take care of children, and make clothes, so meals had to be simple and easy to prepare. They left soups and stews cooking all day while they did other tasks. These dishes were served with flatbreads that were cooked in a pan over the fire or sometimes straight in the **embers**.

Anglo-Saxon women cooked on an open fire inside their home.

Fabulous feasts

On special occasions, such as a victory in battle or a successful hunt, leaders held feasts in the village hall. Everyone in the town was invited, rich and poor, which helped to keep people loyal. For the poorest guests, it was a chance to enjoy generous portions of foods they would not normally be able to afford to eat, such as deer and wild boar. They washed it all down with a honey wine.

WOW!

Anglo-Saxon feasts could go on all day, or even last for several days!

At Anglo-Saxon feasts, people used their knives to pick up pieces of meat, as shown below in this image from the 1000s. Forks weren't commonly used in Britain until the 1700s.

knife picking up food

CLOTHES

GENIUS
★ EYE-CATCHING OUTFITS ★

Making clothes was a role for Anglo-Saxon women, but both men and women took an interest in fashion. They used the resources they had, such as natural dyes and metals, to create colorful, decorated outfits.

Making fabric

The first step in creating clothes was to make the fabric. Anglo-Saxon women used fibers that were easy to come by, such as wool from sheep, and plant fibers, such as flax. They spun these fibers into threads and then wove the threads into pieces of fabric using a **loom**.

Anglo-Saxon clothes were often made from leather (shown below), woven wool fabric, or linen made from plant fibers (shown at right).

Simple designs

Once they had made fabric, women sewed the cloth into clothes. Most Anglo-Saxons couldn't afford clothes for every season and activity, so they dressed in simple garments that were easy to move in and could be layered in cold weather. Men wore trousers, a **tunic**, and a **cloak**. Women typically wore a simple long-sleeved dress with an apron-like garment over top.

The fanciest, most decorated clothes belonged to the richest and most important Anglo-Saxons. These high-ranking men are wearing colored leather straps around their trousers to keep them in place, cloak rings, headbands, and jewelry.

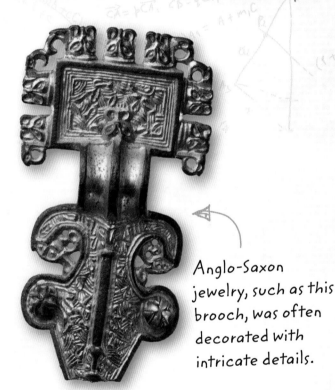

Anglo-Saxon jewelry, such as this brooch, was often decorated with intricate details.

Dazzling details

Although Anglo-Saxon clothes were simple in style, they were often highly decorated. Brightly colored clothes were made by dying fabrics blue, yellow, or red with natural dyes from plants. **Embroidered** details were added on the collars and hems of clothes. Men hung charms and chains from their belts to add interest.

ART

Anglo-Saxon art was heavily decorated with intricate details and repeating patterns. Skilled craftspeople were needed to turn metal, stone, and ivory into impressive pieces of art.

This decorative gold and garnet piece was attached to a sword, where the handle meets the blade. It would have belonged to someone of high status.

Decorating metal

Anglo-Saxon metalworkers used different techniques to turn plain metal items, such as weapon handles, belt buckles, and armor, into beautiful works of art. They shaped fine metal wires into intricate patterns. Glass beads and precious stones, such as garnets, were inlaid to add color.

Rich people wore finely decorated jewelry, such as this pendant.

Christian inspiration

In the 600s, most Anglo-Saxons left behind their **pagan** religion, in which they worshiped many gods, and became Christians. Their new Christian faith inspired their art. They created huge stone crosses, which were placed outside churches. As with their metalwork, they decorated the crosses with patterns, and carved animals, plants, and knotted designs into the stone. They added **inscriptions** in runes, and later in Latin.

Illustrated text

The Anglo-Saxon love of detail and decoration can also be seen in their **illuminated** manuscripts. These are religious texts that are decorated with pictures and fancy writing. **Monks** wrote all of the text in the manuscript by hand, and decorated the pages with colored ink and **gold leaf**. Creating one book could take up to a year.

The highly decorated Bewcastle Cross was made sometime in the 600s or early 700s. It still stands in its original position in the yard of St. Cuthbert's church. The top part of the cross is now missing.

This illuminated manuscript is known as the Lindisfarne Gospels. It is the work of just one monk, named Eadfrith. It took him about 10 years to complete.

(((BRAIN WAVE)))

The monk who created the Lindisfarne Gospels could only use a few local ingredients to make colored inks. However, he cleverly combined the ingredients in different ways to make over ninety different colors! He made purple and blue from **lichen**, yellow from **arsenic**, and white from chalk or crushed shells.

ENTERTAINMENT

Anglo-Saxons had hard and busy lives, but they still found time to have fun. As most people were poor and could not read, they had to come up with creative ways to entertain themselves that didn't depend on reading or spending money.

GENIUS
★ SIMPLE FUN ★

DIY games

Archaeologists have found board games with player pieces and dice in Anglo-Saxon graves. These games were made from cheap materials that were easy to find. Player pieces were stones or pieces of pottery. Dice were made from animal bones. The boards themselves were probably made from wood, so they **decomposed** over time.

Fun at feasts

As well as delicious dishes, guests enjoyed many types of entertainment at feasts. Storytellers told long tales about monsters and heroes, such as Beowulf (see page 29). The guests' creativity and problem-solving skills were put to the test with tricky riddles that they tried to solve together. Can you work out this Anglo-Saxon riddle? *A miracle on the wave / water became bone.* The answer is at the bottom of the page.

This is a modern version of the board game Nine Men's Morris, which was also played by the Anglo-Saxons.

Answer: ice

Making music

Musicians also performed at feasts. They played songs and accompanied storytellers performing stories and poems. This added extra excitement at dramatic points in the tale. Common Anglo-Saxon instruments included the horn, the harp, and the lyre, which is a small harp.

TEST of TIME

Most storytellers didn't write down the stories that they performed, so many Anglo-Saxon tales have been lost. However, the story of Beowulf was written down and survives to this day. The story tells how Beowulf fights against a monster called Grendel. Today, the story is published in books and has been adapted for film and theater.

Feasts had entertainment for all tastes, including clowns, dancers, and jugglers, all accompanied by musicians playing the harp, horns, and the fiddle.

These illustrations from the 1800s were based on Anglo-Saxon drawings.

GLOSSARY

archaeologist A person who studies ancient cultures by examining sites and artifacts

arsenic A metallic element that can be poisonous

Celtic Describes a group of tribes from central Europe, with many settling in Britain, Ireland, and France

Christianity A religion based on the teachings of Jesus Christ

civilization The stage of a human society, such as its culture and way of life

climate The weather conditions in a particular area

cloak A garment worn over clothes, similar to a coat, draped over the shoulders

combat Fighting between individuals or groups

converted To change from one's beliefs or religion to another

culture The beliefs and customs of a group of people

custom A habit or tradition

decomposed Decayed and gradually destroyed

defensive Describes something that is used to protect someone or something from attack

embers Pieces of wood or coal that continue to burn after the flames in a fire have gone out

embroidered To decorate fabric with artful needlework

exile When someone is forced to leave their home and live somewhere else

fertile Soil that is able to produce healthy crops

fortified Made stronger to better defend against attack

gold leaf Gold that has been hammered into a thin sheet

hierarchy A system in which things are organized according to their importance

illuminated A manuscript decorated by hand with gold, silver, or colorful designs

inlaid A decoration or design added to the surface of an object

inscription Words written in or carved onto something

intricate Very complicated or highly detailed

jury A group of people sworn to make a decision in a legal case

legacy Something handed down from the past

lichen A plant found on rocks or trees made from fungus and algae

literacy Being able to read and write

loom A machine used to weave thread into fabric

momentum The strength of a moving object

monk In Christianity, a member of a religious group of men

natural resources Materials or substances from nature that can be used to earn money

nobleman Someone belonging to a high group in society

Old English An Anglo-Saxon language with a largely Germanic vocabulary, used until about 1150

pagan Describes a religion in which people worship many gods

raw material A natural material that has not yet been made into something else

reenactment The staging of or acting out of a past event

rune A letter in the runic alphabet, used by the Anglo-Saxons and other groups in Scandinavia

society A group of people living together in a community

thatched Describes something built using straw or dried plants

tunic A loose garment, often sleeveless, that reaches the knees

Vikings A civilization of seafaring warriors from northern Europe

TIMELINE

410	The Romans leave Britain.
400s	The Anglo-Saxons invade and settle in England.
560	Ethelbert becomes King of Kent. He is the first Anglo-Saxon king to become a Christian.
793	Vikings begin to attack the coast of England, Scotland, and Ireland.
886	King Alfred makes a deal with the Vikings, creating the Danelaw.
925	Athelstan, the first Anglo-Saxon king of the whole of England, is crowned.
1016	Canute, a Viking, becomes king of England.
1042	Edward the Confessor, an Anglo-Saxon, is crowned, replacing the Viking kings.
1066	The Normans defeat the Anglo-Saxons and conquer England.

INDEX

LEARNING MORE

Websites

www.natgeokids.com/uk/discover/history/general-history/anglo-saxons

www.ducksters.com/history/middle_ages/anglo_saxons.php

www.dkfindout.com/us/history/anglo-saxons/

Books

Gifford, Clive. *Anglo-Saxon and Viking Times.* Wayland, 2017.

Mason, Paul. *The Anglo-Saxons are Coming.* Franklin Watts, 2018.

Richardson, Hazel. *Life of the Ancient Vikings.* Crabtree Publishing, 2005.